We hope this book has been informative and helpful on your journey to understanding and celebrating older adults. Thank you for your interest and support!

AF378034

Title: The Tactical Minds of Football
Subtitle: A Close Look at the Coaching Strategies of Three Legends

Series: The Masterminds of Football: Biographies & Memoirs

By Chester Madison

"The most important thing is to win, not just to play good football."
Pep Guardiola, Manchester City Manager

"If you want to be a champion, you have to score more goals than the opponent."
Jose Mourinho, AS Roma Manager

"It's not just about winning, it's about winning with style."
Arsène Wenger, Former Arsenal Manager

"The difference between a successful person and others is not a lack of strength, not a lack of knowledge, but rather a lack of will."
Vince Lombardi, Former American Football Coach (this quote is often used in football as well)

"In football, the result is an impostor. You can do things really, really well but not win. There's something greater than the result, more lasting - a legacy."
Xavi, Former Barcelona Midfielder

"The ball is the most important thing. It's the only thing that never gets tired."

Jürgen Klopp, Liverpool Manager

"I don't believe skill was, or ever will be, the result of coaches. It is a result of a love affair between the child and the ball."
Roy Keane, Former Manchester United Midfielder

"Football is not just about winning, it's about playing with passion and giving your best every time you step onto the pitch."
Diego Simeone, Atlético Madrid Manager

Table of Contents

Introduction

Overview of the book

"The Tactical Minds of Football" is a book that examines the careers of three of the greatest football coaches of all time - Guus Hiddink, Roy Hodgson, and Carlos Bilardo. These coaches have each had remarkable careers in football, with achievements that span across several decades.

This book aims to provide an in-depth look into the coaching philosophies and tactical strategies of these three coaches, and how they have influenced the sport. The book will provide readers with an understanding of the key characteristics that made these coaches successful, and how their approaches to coaching can be applied in the modern game.

In this book, we will examine each coach's early life and career, their most significant achievements, their coaching styles and philosophies, and their legacies in the sport. Through this analysis, we aim to provide readers with a comprehensive understanding of the unique coaching approaches that each of these great coaches employed.

It is important to note that this book is not a biography of these coaches but rather a study of their coaching philosophies and tactics. While we will touch on their personal lives and careers, the primary focus will be on their contributions to the sport of football and how their legacies have influenced the game.

This book is intended for anyone interested in football, from coaches and players to avid fans of the sport. It is our hope that by examining the careers of these great coaches, readers will gain insight into the game's tactical side and develop a deeper appreciation for the coaches' role in football.

Overall, "The Tactical Minds of Football" provides a unique and insightful look into the careers of three of the greatest football coaches of all time, examining their tactical minds, coaching philosophies, and legacies. We hope that readers will find this book informative, engaging, and valuable in understanding the sport of football.

Importance of the coaches in football

Coaches play a critical role in the success of any football team. They are responsible for developing tactical strategies, managing players' physical and mental well-being, and providing leadership on and off the field. In this section, we will explore the importance of coaches in football and their impact on the sport.

Coaches have a significant impact on a team's tactical approach. They are responsible for developing and implementing game plans that take into account the strengths and weaknesses of their team and their opponents. A good coach can transform a mediocre team into a winning one by devising effective tactics and strategies.

Coaches also have a crucial role in managing their players' physical and mental well-being. They must ensure that their players are physically fit and healthy, able to perform to the best of their abilities. They must also provide support and guidance to their players, helping them to navigate the challenges of a high-pressure sport.

In addition to their tactical and managerial responsibilities, coaches also serve as role models for their players. They set the tone for the team's culture and values, and their leadership can inspire players to give their best efforts on and off the field.

Moreover, coaches can be instrumental in developing young players and bringing them through the ranks. By providing guidance and mentorship, coaches can help young players develop their skills and fulfill their potential, contributing to the long-term success of a team.

The impact of coaches extends beyond the success of individual teams. They also play a critical role in shaping the sport of football. The tactical innovations and strategies developed by great coaches have influenced the game's evolution and development. Their legacies have inspired future generations of coaches to push the boundaries of what is possible on the field.

In conclusion, coaches are essential to the success of any football team. They are responsible for developing tactical strategies, managing players' physical and mental well-being, and providing leadership on and off the field. Their impact extends beyond individual teams and has contributed to the development and evolution of the sport. The coaches in this book are prime examples of the crucial role coaches play in the world of football.

In this section, we will provide a brief background on the three coaches featured in this book: Guus Hiddink, Roy Hodgson, and Carlos Bilardo. Each of these coaches has had a significant impact on the sport of football and has made lasting contributions to the teams and players they have coached.

Guus Hiddink is a Dutch football coach who has worked with a number of high-profile teams and national teams over his career. Hiddink started his coaching career in the Netherlands in the early 1980s, coaching several Eredivisie teams before leading PSV Eindhoven to European glory in 1988. He later went on to coach the Dutch national team, leading them to the semi-finals of the 1998 World Cup. Hiddink has also coached a number of other national teams, including South Korea, Australia, and Russia, and has had stints at several high-profile clubs, including Chelsea, Real Madrid, and Anzhi Makhachkala.

Roy Hodgson is an English football coach who has worked with several teams and national teams over his career. Hodgson began his coaching career in Sweden in the late 1970s, coaching several teams before leading Halmstads BK to two Swedish championships. He later coached several other European teams, including Inter Milan, where he won the UEFA Cup in 1998. Hodgson has also coached a number of national teams, including Switzerland, Finland, and England. He has had stints at several high-profile clubs, including Liverpool, Fulham, and Crystal Palace.

Carlos Bilardo is an Argentine football coach who has had a significant impact on the sport both as a player and a coach. Bilardo began his playing career in Argentina in the 1960s before moving to Spain to play for Sevilla. He later returned to Argentina, where he played for Estudiantes de La Plata and helped them win several titles. Bilardo then transitioned to coaching, leading Estudiantes de La Plata to three Argentine championships and the 1983 Copa Libertadores. He later coached the Argentine national team, leading them to World Cup victory in 1986. Bilardo has also coached several clubs in Spain and Colombia and has served as a mentor and advisor to many other coaches throughout his career.

In this book, we will explore the coaching philosophies, strategies, and legacies of these three great coaches. Each has had a unique approach to coaching and has left a lasting impact on the teams and players they have worked with. We will examine their careers in detail, providing insights into their successes, challenges, and the lessons that can be learned from their experiences.

Objective of the book

The objective of this book is to provide an in-depth look at the careers of three great football coaches: Guus Hiddink, Roy Hodgson, and Carlos Bilardo. Each of these coaches has had a significant impact on the sport of football and has made lasting contributions to the teams and players they have coached.

Through detailed analysis of their careers, coaching philosophies, and strategies, we aim to provide readers with valuable insights into the world of football coaching. Our objective is to help readers better understand the complexities of football coaching, from the tactical decisions that are made on the field to the interpersonal relationships that must be managed off the field.

We will examine the key moments in each coach's career, from their early years as coaches to their most recent achievements. We will explore their approaches to training and development, their strategies for game preparation, and their techniques for motivating and inspiring players.

In addition to providing a detailed look at each coach's career, our objective is to provide readers with practical advice and guidance that can be applied to their own coaching efforts. We will highlight key lessons learned from the careers of these coaches, and provide insights into how these lessons can be applied in a variety of coaching contexts.

Ultimately, our objective is to provide readers with a comprehensive understanding of the art and science of football coaching, as seen through the eyes of three of the greatest coaches in the sport's history. Whether you are a seasoned coach looking to refine your skills or a novice coach just starting out, we believe that this book will provide you with valuable insights, practical advice, and inspiration to help you achieve your coaching goals.

Guus Hiddink was born on November 8, 1946, in Varsseveld, a small town in the eastern Netherlands. Hiddink grew up in a family of farmers, and he initially planned to follow in his father's footsteps and work on the family farm. However, Hiddink's passion for football soon became evident, and he began playing for the local club, Varsseveldse Boys, at a young age.

Hiddink's talent as a football player was evident from an early age, and he quickly began to attract the attention of scouts from professional clubs. In 1967, Hiddink was signed by De Graafschap, a professional club in the Netherlands' second division. Hiddink played as a midfielder, and he quickly became a key player for De Graafschap, helping the club win promotion to the first division in 1969.

After four seasons with De Graafschap, Hiddink moved to NEC Nijmegen, where he played for two seasons before retiring from playing in 1982 at the age of 35.

Throughout his playing career, Hiddink had already begun to develop an interest in coaching, and he had taken on various coaching roles with amateur and youth teams. In 1982, he was appointed as head coach of De Graafschap, the club where he had begun his playing career.

Hiddink's early years as a coach were challenging, as he struggled to establish himself as a respected and successful coach. However, he persevered, and he gradually began to build a reputation as a talented and innovative coach.

In 1987, Hiddink was appointed as head coach of PSV Eindhoven, one of the most successful clubs in Dutch football. Hiddink's time at PSV would prove to be the defining period of his coaching career, as he led the club to a string of domestic and international successes.

In the next section, we will explore Hiddink's early coaching experiences, including his time at De Graafschap, and how these experiences shaped his coaching philosophy and approach to the game.

First coaching experiences

After retiring from playing in 1982, Guus Hiddink immediately began to pursue a career in coaching. He was appointed as head coach of De Graafschap, the club where he had begun his playing career, and he set about implementing his vision for the team.

Hiddink's early years as a coach were challenging, as he struggled to establish himself as a respected and successful coach. However, he persevered, and he gradually began to build a reputation as a talented and innovative coach.

At De Graafschap, Hiddink implemented a number of changes that would set the tone for his coaching philosophy for years to come. He emphasized the importance of fitness, discipline, and tactical awareness, and he demanded a high level of commitment and professionalism from his players.

Under Hiddink's leadership, De Graafschap began to improve both on and off the pitch. The team's performances on the pitch were more consistent, and they began to climb the league table. Off the pitch, Hiddink implemented a number of changes to the club's infrastructure, including improving the training facilities and investing in youth development.

Hiddink's success at De Graafschap caught the attention of other clubs, and he was soon offered the opportunity to coach at higher levels. In 1984, he was appointed as head coach of FC Emmen, a club in the Netherlands' second division.

Hiddink's time at FC Emmen was short-lived, as he was soon offered the opportunity to coach at one of the biggest clubs in Dutch football. In 1987, he was appointed as head coach of PSV Eindhoven, one of the most successful clubs in Dutch football.

At PSV, Hiddink continued to build on the foundation he had established at De Graafschap. He emphasized the importance of tactical awareness and team cohesion, and he worked tirelessly to improve his players' fitness and technical skills.

Under Hiddink's leadership, PSV enjoyed a period of sustained success, winning a string of domestic and international trophies. In 1988, they won the Dutch league title, and in 1989, they reached the final of the European Cup, where they were narrowly defeated by AC Milan.

Hiddink's success at PSV established him as one of the most talented coaches in Dutch football, and he was soon offered the opportunity to coach at the international level. In the next section, we will explore Hiddink's time coaching the

Dutch national team, and the impact he had on the team's fortunes.

Leading PSV to European glory

Guus Hiddink's success with PSV Eindhoven in the late 1980s was a defining moment in his coaching career. After stints with De Graafschap and NEC Nijmegen, Hiddink took over at PSV in 1987. At the time, the club had not won the Eredivisie title in four years, and Hiddink was tasked with restoring the team's winning ways.

Under Hiddink's leadership, PSV achieved immediate success. In his first season, he led the club to a domestic league and cup double, and the following year, they won the European Cup by defeating Benfica on penalties in the final. Hiddink's tactical acumen was on full display during the European Cup run, as he masterminded victories over Real Madrid and Bordeaux in the knockout stages.

Hiddink's success with PSV was not only due to his tactical acumen, but also his man-management skills. He built a team around the talented attacking trio of Ronald Koeman, Wim Kieft, and Gerald Vanenburg, while also developing promising young players such as Ruud Gullit and Eric Gerets.

Hiddink's tenure at PSV was marked by a commitment to attacking football, with an emphasis on possession and fluid movement. He was also known for his attention to detail, with a focus on set-piece routines and individual player development.

The success Hiddink achieved at PSV paved the way for future coaching opportunities, both domestically and internationally. His achievements with the club are still remembered today, and he is regarded as one of the greatest coaches in PSV's history.

Overall, Hiddink's time at PSV demonstrated his ability to lead a team to success on the domestic and international stage, and established him as one of the most promising coaches of his generation.

Coaching the Dutch national team

Guus Hiddink's coaching career has been defined by his ability to achieve success at both the club and international levels. One of the most significant international roles Hiddink held was as the head coach of the Dutch national team.

Hiddink took over as head coach of the Netherlands in 1994, following the team's disappointing performance at the World Cup in the United States. His first major tournament with the team was the 1996 European Championship, which was hosted by England.

The Netherlands had a strong showing in the tournament, finishing in third place. Hiddink's tactical acumen was again on full display, as he deployed a 3-4-3 formation that allowed the team's talented attackers to flourish. Dennis Bergkamp, who was a key member of Hiddink's team, praised the coach for his ability to get the best out of his players.

Hiddink's success with the Dutch national team continued into the 1998 World Cup in France. The team, which featured stars such as Bergkamp, Frank de Boer, and Edgar Davids, made it to the semifinals before losing to Brazil in a penalty shootout. The team's attacking prowess was again evident, as they scored 13 goals in their six matches.

Following the World Cup, Hiddink left his role as head coach of the Netherlands to take on a new challenge: leading the South Korean national team. However, he would return to the Dutch national team for a second stint in 2014, leading the team to the semifinals of the World Cup in Brazil.

Hiddink's success with the Dutch national team can be attributed to his tactical flexibility and man-management skills. He was able to get the best out of some of the world's most talented players, while also developing a system of play that allowed the team to attack with precision and flair.

Overall, Hiddink's time as head coach of the Dutch national team is a testament to his ability to lead a team to success at the international level. His tactical acumen and man-management skills have made him one of the most successful coaches in the history of the game.

Stints at various clubs

Guus Hiddink's success with PSV Eindhoven caught the attention of several top clubs, and he went on to manage several prominent teams throughout his career. Here's a look at some of his notable stints at various clubs:

1. Fenerbahçe (1990-1991): Hiddink's first stint abroad was with the Turkish club Fenerbahçe, where he won the Turkish Cup in his first season. However, he left the club after just one year due to financial disagreements with the board.

2. Valencia (1991-1994): Hiddink's next stop was at Spanish club Valencia, where he led them to their first European final in 24 years in the 1991-92 season. They lost to Werder Bremen in the UEFA Cup final, but Hiddink's impact was clear. He won the Copa del Rey in his first season and helped Valencia finish third in La Liga in his second season.

3. Netherlands (1995-1998): Hiddink returned to his home country to coach the Dutch national team again, this time for the 1998 World Cup. He led them to the semi-finals, where they lost to Brazil on penalties.

4. Real Madrid (1998-1999): Hiddink took charge of Real Madrid for the 1998-99 season, but it was a turbulent year for the club. They finished fifth in La Liga, and Hiddink

resigned after just one season due to disagreements with the club's hierarchy.

5. Real Betis (1999-2000): Hiddink returned to Spain to manage Real Betis, but it was a short-lived stint. He resigned midway through the season due to disagreements with the board.

6. South Korea (2001-2002): Hiddink's most notable international coaching success came with South Korea at the 2002 World Cup. He led them to the semi-finals, where they lost to Germany, but their run captured the imagination of the football world.

7. Australia (2005): Hiddink led Australia to the 2006 World Cup after taking over midway through the qualification campaign. He helped them secure their first World Cup appearance in 32 years.

8. Chelsea (2009): Hiddink returned to club management in 2009, taking over as interim manager at Chelsea after the sacking of Luiz Felipe Scolari. He led the team to an FA Cup win that season, but declined to stay on permanently.

Throughout his various stints at clubs, Hiddink's ability to get the best out of his players and his tactical nous stood out. He often implemented a flexible 4-3-3 formation that could adapt to different opponents and situations.

Hiddink's successes at both club and international level cemented his status as one of the most respected coaches in the game.

Guus Hiddink is widely recognized for his successful stints as a coach for various football clubs and national teams, including PSV Eindhoven, the Dutch national team, and South Korea. His coaching style and philosophy have been integral to his success, and have also influenced other coaches in the sport.

Hiddink is known for his tactical flexibility, adapting his strategies to the strengths and weaknesses of his team and the opposition. He is also known for his focus on team unity and the development of a strong team culture. Hiddink has emphasized the importance of communication and building relationships with players, creating an environment of trust and mutual respect. This has allowed him to create a sense of ownership and responsibility among his players, encouraging them to take initiative and make decisions on the pitch.

Hiddink's coaching philosophy is based on the belief that football is a collective sport that requires a strong team ethic. He has emphasized the importance of team cohesion, and has often prioritized team performance over individual achievement. Hiddink has also stressed the importance of a strong work ethic, discipline, and attention to detail.

Another key aspect of Hiddink's coaching style is his ability to motivate his players. He has a talent for creating a positive and energizing atmosphere that inspires his players to give their best efforts. Hiddink has also been known to be a calming presence, providing stability and reassurance during high-pressure situations.

Hiddink's coaching style and philosophy have been instrumental in his success. His teams have consistently performed well, achieving notable victories in both domestic and international competitions. His approach has also earned him the respect of his players, colleagues, and fans, making him one of the most highly-regarded coaches in the world.

In summary, Hiddink's coaching style and philosophy emphasize tactical flexibility, team unity, communication, motivation, and a strong work ethic. His ability to adapt to different situations and create a positive team culture have been integral to his success as a coach. Hiddink's influence on football coaching can be seen in the strategies and philosophies of many other successful coaches in the sport.

Roy Hodgson is a football manager with a wealth of experience in the sport. He was born on August 9, 1947, in Croydon, England. Hodgson had a difficult childhood, as his father was a bus driver who was frequently absent from the family home. Despite these challenges, Hodgson showed an early talent for football and began playing for local youth teams.

Hodgson's first professional club was Crystal Palace, where he played as a defender. He spent several years at the club before moving to Maidstone United in 1969. After a season at Maidstone, he moved to South Africa to play for Berea Park. Hodgson enjoyed success in South Africa, winning the National Professional Soccer League with the club in 1971.

After three years in South Africa, Hodgson returned to England to play for Bristol City. He also had brief spells at Stoke City and Southampton before retiring from playing in 1980.

After retiring as a player, Hodgson began his coaching career. His first coaching job was at Halmstad in Sweden, where he won the Swedish league title twice. He then moved to Switzerland, where he won the Swiss Super League with FC Neuchatel Xamax in 1988.

In 1992, Hodgson returned to England to manage Blackburn Rovers. He led the club to promotion to the Premier League in his first season in charge. After four seasons at Blackburn, Hodgson had brief spells at several clubs, including Inter Milan, Grasshoppers, and FC Copenhagen.

In 2006, Hodgson became manager of the Finland national team. He led the team to their highest ever FIFA ranking of 33rd in the world. In 2007, Hodgson returned to England to manage Fulham. He led the club to the UEFA Europa League final in 2010, where they were narrowly beaten by Atletico Madrid.

Hodgson's success at Fulham earned him the job as manager of the England national team in 2012. He led the team to the quarter-finals of the 2012 European Championships and the 2014 World Cup, but his tenure was ultimately considered a disappointment due to England's early exit in both tournaments.

Throughout his career, Hodgson has gained a reputation for being a thoughtful and meticulous coach. He is known for his emphasis on defensive organization and his ability to get the best out of his players. His experience and success in different countries and with different teams have made him one of the most respected coaches in football.

Coaching in Sweden and Switzerland

Roy Hodgson's early coaching career saw him work in various countries, including Sweden and Switzerland, where he gained valuable experience and honed his coaching skills.

After a brief stint as a player, Hodgson began his coaching career at Halmstads BK in Sweden in 1976. At the time, Halmstads BK was a mid-table team in the Swedish first division, and Hodgson was tasked with turning the club's fortunes around. Under his guidance, Halmstads BK gradually improved and won their first-ever league title in 1979, shocking the footballing world.

Hodgson then moved to another Swedish club, Örebro SK, where he continued his successful run, leading them to a top-three finish in the league. His success in Sweden did not go unnoticed, and he was offered the head coach role at FC Zurich in Switzerland in 1980.

At FC Zurich, Hodgson continued to impress, leading the club to a Swiss Cup victory in his first season. He also took the team to the semi-finals of the UEFA Cup, where they narrowly lost to eventual winners IFK Göteborg. Hodgson's tactical acumen and attention to detail were evident during his time at FC Zurich, and his success with the club earned him the opportunity to coach the Swiss national team.

Hodgson's time as the Swiss national team coach was relatively short, but he managed to make an impact, leading the team to their first major tournament in nearly three decades. Switzerland qualified for the 1994 World Cup under his guidance, and Hodgson's tactical nous was on full display during the tournament, as he helped the Swiss secure a historic 4-1 win over Romania.

In conclusion, Hodgson's early coaching experiences in Sweden and Switzerland were instrumental in shaping his career as a football manager. He proved himself as a tactical mastermind and a coach who could turn around the fortunes of struggling teams. His success in these countries earned him opportunities at higher levels of the game, and he went on to achieve great success in other countries as well.

Hodgson's success with Inter Milan

In 1995, Roy Hodgson was appointed as the manager of Inter Milan. This was a big move for Hodgson, as Inter Milan was one of the biggest football clubs in Europe. At the time, Inter Milan was struggling and had not won a major trophy in almost a decade. Hodgson's appointment was seen as a surprise, but he quickly proved his worth by leading Inter Milan to one of their most successful seasons in recent memory.

Hodgson's first season at Inter Milan was a mixed bag. The team finished in seventh place in Serie A, but Hodgson managed to lead them to the UEFA Cup final. Unfortunately, they lost the final to Schalke 04. However, Hodgson's success in the UEFA Cup was a sign of things to come.

The following season, Hodgson led Inter Milan to their first European trophy in almost a decade. They won the UEFA Cup, beating Lazio in the final. The victory was seen as a huge achievement for Hodgson and for Inter Milan. Hodgson's tactical acumen and ability to get the best out of his players were key factors in the team's success.

Hodgson's success with Inter Milan was not limited to just the UEFA Cup. He also led the team to a third-place finish in Serie A, which was their best finish in years. The team was competitive and played attractive football, which was a big departure from the defensive style of play that had been employed in previous years.

Hodgson's success with Inter Milan made him one of the most respected managers in Europe. He had shown that he was capable of leading a big club to success and had done so with a team that had been struggling. His ability to develop and implement tactical plans, as well as his man-management skills, were key factors in his success at Inter Milan.

Overall, Hodgson's success with Inter Milan was a testament to his abilities as a manager. He had taken a struggling team and turned them into one of the best teams in Europe. His success at Inter Milan paved the way for future managerial roles at Blackburn Rovers, Fulham, and eventually the England national team.

National team coaching experiences

Roy Hodgson's success at the club level brought him to the attention of national teams. He has coached several national teams during his career, each with varying degrees of success. In this section, we will look at his experiences coaching national teams and the impact he had on them.

1. Switzerland Hodgson's first foray into international management came in 1992 when he took over the Swiss national team. Switzerland had not qualified for a major tournament since the 1960s, but Hodgson quickly turned their fortunes around. He guided them to the 1994 World Cup, their first major tournament in nearly 30 years. Switzerland went on to reach the round of 16, where they were knocked out by Spain.

2. United Arab Emirates After leaving Switzerland, Hodgson had a brief stint managing the United Arab Emirates national team. He was appointed in 2002 but resigned less than a year later due to a lack of support from the country's football association.

3. Finland In 2005, Hodgson was appointed as the manager of the Finland national team. This was a significant challenge, as Finland had never qualified for a major tournament before. However, Hodgson's tactical acumen and attention to detail helped them improve dramatically.

Under his leadership, Finland climbed to their highest ever FIFA ranking of 33rd. They narrowly missed out on qualification for Euro 2008, finishing third in their group behind Portugal and Poland.

4. England In 2012, Hodgson was appointed as the manager of the England national team. This was the pinnacle of his career, as England is one of the most prestigious national teams in the world. However, Hodgson's time in charge of England was somewhat controversial. He was criticized for his cautious tactics and failure to get the best out of his players. Despite this, he did guide England to the quarter-finals of Euro 2012 and the 2014 World Cup.

5. Crystal Palace After leaving the England job, Hodgson returned to club management with Crystal Palace. However, he still had one more stint with a national team in him. In 2018, he was appointed as the manager of the Swedish national team. This was somewhat unexpected, as Hodgson had no previous connection to Sweden. However, he was able to guide them to the quarter-finals of the 2018 World Cup, their best performance in the tournament since 1994.

Overall, Hodgson's national team coaching experiences demonstrate his versatility and ability to adapt to different environments. He was able to guide Switzerland

and Finland to their first major tournaments in decades, while also leading England and Sweden to respectable performances on the international stage.

After spending time coaching in different countries, Hodgson returned to England to take charge of several Premier League clubs. His experiences in England were a mixed bag, but he managed to make his mark on the English football landscape.

Fulham:

Hodgson's first job in England was at Fulham in 2007, where he took over from Lawrie Sanchez. He managed to keep the club in the Premier League in his first season in charge, and in his second season, he led Fulham to their highest-ever finish of seventh place, qualifying for the Europa League. Hodgson's tactical acumen was on full display during Fulham's Europa League run, where they made it all the way to the final, only to lose to Atletico Madrid in extra time. Despite the loss, Hodgson's achievement with Fulham was widely praised.

Liverpool:

After his success at Fulham, Hodgson was appointed as the manager of Liverpool in July 2010. However, his tenure at Liverpool was short-lived and largely unsuccessful. He struggled to get the team playing the way he wanted, and the results on the pitch were poor. Hodgson's reign at

Liverpool ended in January 2011, with the team languishing in the bottom half of the Premier League table.

West Bromwich Albion:

After leaving Liverpool, Hodgson was appointed as the manager of West Bromwich Albion in February 2011. He managed to keep the club in the Premier League in his first season in charge, and in his second season, he led West Brom to their highest-ever Premier League finish of eighth place. Hodgson's ability to get the best out of his players was evident during his time at West Brom, and he was widely praised for his work at the club.

Crystal Palace:

Hodgson's last job in English football was at Crystal Palace, where he was appointed as the manager in September 2017. He managed to keep the club in the Premier League in his first season in charge, and in his second season, he led Crystal Palace to their highest-ever Premier League points total of 49. Hodgson's ability to organize his team and make them difficult to beat was once again on full display during his time at Crystal Palace.

Hodgson's Coaching Style and Philosophy:

Hodgson is known for his emphasis on defensive organization and discipline. He often sets his teams up to be difficult to break down, with a focus on keeping a solid shape and limiting the opposition's opportunities. Hodgson's teams are also known for their ability to hit on the counter-attack, with fast and direct attacking play.

In terms of player management, Hodgson is known for his ability to get the best out of his players, particularly those who are not necessarily the most talented. He is a master at identifying a player's strengths and weaknesses and setting up his team to maximize those strengths while minimizing their weaknesses.

Overall, Hodgson's coaching style and philosophy have been effective at various stages of his career. While he has had his ups and downs, he has always been able to adapt to his team's strengths and weaknesses and find a way to get results.

Hodgson's approach to coaching and management

Roy Hodgson is known for his calm and measured approach to coaching and management. He has often been praised for his ability to bring stability to teams, especially those in crisis, and for his tactical acumen.

One of Hodgson's key strengths as a coach is his attention to detail. He is known for his meticulous preparation for matches, analyzing every aspect of the opposition's play and formulating a plan to nullify their strengths and exploit their weaknesses. He is also very focused on his own team's performance, ensuring that each player understands their role and the team's overall strategy.

Hodgson is also known for his ability to communicate with players and create a positive team environment. He is seen as a good motivator, with a particular talent for instilling confidence in players who may be lacking in self-belief. His calm demeanor and measured approach to management have also been praised as helping to reduce pressure on players and create a more relaxed atmosphere in the dressing room.

In terms of tactics, Hodgson is known for his preference for a well-organized and disciplined defensive structure. He often employs a deep-lying defensive line, looking to frustrate opposition attacks and then hit on the counter-attack. He also places a strong emphasis on set-piece routines, recognizing the importance of these moments in tight matches.

Despite his reputation as a defensive-minded coach, Hodgson has shown himself capable of adapting to different situations and playing styles. During his time at Fulham, he led the team to a Europa League final playing an attacking and possession-based style, while at Crystal Palace, he introduced a more aggressive and high-pressing approach.

Overall, Hodgson's approach to coaching and management can be characterized as highly professional, meticulous, and focused on creating a positive team environment. His tactical acumen and ability to adapt to different situations have made him a highly respected figure in the world of football coaching.

Carlos Bilardo is one of the most respected and accomplished football coaches in Argentine history. Born on March 16, 1939, in Buenos Aires, he grew up in the Villa Devoto neighborhood of the city. Bilardo's passion for football started at a young age, and he played for various amateur teams before joining the youth academy of San Lorenzo de Almagro.

After completing his studies as a doctor, Bilardo began his professional football career as a player for Estudiantes de La Plata in 1960. He played as a defender and was part of the team that won the 1967 Metropolitan Championship. He retired as a player in 1970 after suffering a serious injury.

After his playing days were over, Bilardo turned to coaching. He started with various amateur teams in Buenos Aires before being hired as the coach of Estudiantes in 1975. It was during this time that he developed his reputation for being a tough and demanding coach. He instilled a strong work ethic in his players and was known for his attention to detail and meticulous planning.

Under Bilardo's leadership, Estudiantes won the Metropolitano Championship in 1982 and the Nacional

Championship in 1983. However, Bilardo's most significant achievement as a coach came when he led the Argentine national team to victory in the 1986 World Cup.

Bilardo's success with the national team was due in part to his ability to motivate and inspire his players. He created a strong team spirit and emphasized the importance of playing as a unit. He also employed innovative tactics, such as the "five-man defense" that allowed Argentina to neutralize opposing teams' attacking threats while also creating scoring opportunities on the counter-attack.

After winning the World Cup, Bilardo continued to coach the national team until 1990, when Argentina reached the final of the World Cup but lost to West Germany. He then went on to coach various clubs in Argentina and Colombia, including Boca Juniors, San Lorenzo de Almagro, and Deportivo Cali.

Throughout his career, Bilardo was known for his intense focus and dedication to the game. He was a student of the sport and spent countless hours studying tactics and analyzing opposing teams. He was also a disciplinarian who demanded the highest standards from his players.

In summary, Carlos Bilardo's early life and career were characterized by his passion for football and his success as a player for Estudiantes de La Plata. However, it was his achievements as a coach, particularly leading the Argentine national team to victory in the 1986 World Cup, that cemented his legacy as one of the greatest football coaches of all time. Bilardo's attention to detail, innovative tactics, and unwavering commitment to excellence continue to inspire football coaches around the world.

Carlos Bilardo is widely regarded as one of the most successful coaches in Argentinian football history. His career spanned over four decades, during which he led several teams to domestic and international success. One of his most notable achievements was leading Estudiantes de La Plata to three consecutive Copa Libertadores titles in the late 1960s.

Bilardo began his playing career as a defender for the Argentinian club San Lorenzo in the early 1960s. However, it was his coaching career that would make him a household name in Argentinian football. He began coaching Estudiantes de La Plata in 1970 and quickly made his mark by winning the Metropolitano championship in 1971.

Bilardo's biggest achievement with Estudiantes came between 1968 and 1970 when he led them to three consecutive Copa Libertadores titles. The Copa Libertadores is South America's premier club competition and is equivalent to the UEFA Champions League in Europe. Estudiantes' victories were notable for their physical and combative style of play, which was often described as "ugly" but highly effective.

Bilardo's tactics were based on a strong emphasis on defense and counter-attacking football. He believed in a highly disciplined and organized approach, with an emphasis on team spirit and unity. His teams were known for their physicality and tenacity, which made them difficult to beat.

Bilardo's success with Estudiantes paved the way for a highly successful coaching career. He went on to manage several teams in Argentina, including Boca Juniors, San Lorenzo, and Deportivo Español. He also managed the Argentinian national team, leading them to victory in the 1986 World Cup, which is widely regarded as one of the greatest achievements in Argentinian football history.

Bilardo's success as a coach was not just down to his tactical nous, but also his ability to motivate his players. He was known for his tough, no-nonsense approach and his uncompromising nature. His man-management skills were highly regarded, and he was known for his ability to get the best out of his players.

In conclusion, Carlos Bilardo's early success with Estudiantes de La Plata set the tone for a highly successful coaching career. His disciplined and combative approach to football, coupled with his excellent man-management skills, made him one of the most successful coaches in Argentinian football history.

Coaching the Argentine national team

Carlos Bilardo is known as one of the most influential coaches in the history of Argentine football. He is most famous for leading the Argentine national team to their second World Cup victory in 1986. In this chapter, we will discuss Bilardo's coaching career, with a specific focus on his time as the coach of the Argentine national team.

Bilardo's coaching career began in the mid-1970s, when he took over as coach of Estudiantes de La Plata. At the time, Estudiantes was struggling in the Argentine first division, but Bilardo quickly turned the team's fortunes around. In 1977, Estudiantes won their first Argentine league title in almost a decade, and Bilardo was hailed as a hero by the club's fans.

Bilardo's success with Estudiantes was built on his meticulous attention to detail and his innovative tactical approach. He was one of the first coaches in Argentina to use video analysis as a coaching tool, and he was also known for his rigorous fitness programs. Bilardo believed that success on the field was built on a foundation of hard work and preparation, and he instilled these values in his players.

After leaving Estudiantes, Bilardo took over as coach of the Argentine national team in 1982. His tenure got off to a rocky start, with the team struggling in the early stages of qualifying for the 1986 World Cup. However, Bilardo's meticulous approach eventually paid off, and the team qualified for the tournament with a game to spare.

At the 1986 World Cup, Bilardo's Argentine team played some of the most exciting and innovative football of the tournament. Bilardo's tactics were built around the genius of Diego Maradona, who he deployed in a deep-lying playmaker role that allowed him to roam freely and create scoring opportunities for his teammates. The team's attacking play was complemented by a rock-solid defense, which conceded just five goals in seven games.

In the final against West Germany, Bilardo's team showed their resilience and tactical nous, coming from behind to win 3-2. The victory cemented Bilardo's place in Argentine football folklore and established him as one of the greatest coaches in the history of the game.

After the World Cup victory, Bilardo continued to coach the Argentine national team until 1990, when he stepped down following a disappointing performance at the World Cup in Italy. He went on to coach several clubs in Argentina and Mexico, but he was never able to replicate the success he had with the national team.

Throughout his coaching career, Bilardo was known for his tactical acumen and his meticulous attention to detail.

He was a coach who demanded the highest standards from his players, both on and off the field, and he believed that success was built on a foundation of hard work and preparation. His approach to coaching was influential not just in Argentina, but around the world, and his legacy continues to be felt in the game today.

Bilardo's tactics and strategies

Carlos Bilardo is widely regarded as one of the most innovative and tactical coaches in the history of football. Throughout his career, he developed a number of tactics and strategies that helped his teams to succeed on the field.

One of Bilardo's most notable tactical innovations was his implementation of a 3-5-2 formation. This formation, which features three central defenders, five midfielders, and two strikers, was a departure from the more traditional 4-4-2 formation that was commonly used at the time. Bilardo's 3-5-2 formation was designed to give his teams greater defensive stability and control in midfield, while also allowing them to attack with greater numbers.

Another key aspect of Bilardo's tactical approach was his emphasis on team discipline and organization. He believed that a team could only be successful if every player was committed to working hard and following the coach's instructions. To this end, he placed a great deal of emphasis on defensive organization and pressing, encouraging his teams to press high up the pitch and win the ball back quickly.

Bilardo was also known for his attention to detail and meticulous preparation. He was a keen student of the game and spent hours studying his opponents and analyzing their strengths and weaknesses. He would then use this information to develop specific game plans and strategies that would allow his team to exploit their opponent's weaknesses and neutralize their strengths.

One example of Bilardo's attention to detail was his use of pre-match routines and rituals. He would have his players perform a series of exercises and drills before every game, with each exercise designed to help the team focus and prepare mentally and physically for the challenges ahead.

Bilardo's tactical innovations and attention to detail helped him to achieve great success as a coach, both at club and international level. His Argentine national team, which won the 1986 World Cup, is widely regarded as one of the greatest teams in the history of football, and his influence on the game is still felt today.

Coaching experiences in Spain and Colombia

Carlos Bilardo is a legendary coach from Argentina who has coached several clubs and national teams across different countries. After his stint with the Argentine national team, Bilardo went on to coach teams in Spain and Colombia, leaving a significant impact on the football scene in these countries.

Coaching in Spain

Bilardo's first coaching experience outside Argentina came in 1992, when he was appointed as the head coach of Sevilla FC in Spain. Sevilla had been struggling in the league and were looking for a coach who could help them turn their fortunes around. Bilardo's arrival at the club was greeted with much enthusiasm, and the fans were hopeful that he would be able to guide the team to success.

Bilardo's coaching style was different from that of his predecessors at Sevilla. He emphasized a more defensive approach, which focused on keeping the team organized at the back and hitting on the counter-attack. This approach proved to be effective, as Sevilla managed to win several games that they had previously struggled to win.

In Bilardo's first season at the club, Sevilla finished in a respectable sixth place in La Liga, which was a significant improvement from their previous season's performance.

However, his second season at the club was not as successful, as Sevilla struggled to replicate their previous season's form and finished in twelfth place in the league. Bilardo was subsequently dismissed from his role as the head coach of Sevilla.

Despite his relatively short stint with Sevilla, Bilardo's impact on the club was significant. He had introduced a new style of play, which helped the team win games they would have otherwise lost. Additionally, he had also helped to develop several young players, who would go on to become important players for the club in the future.

Coaching in Colombia

After his stint with Sevilla, Bilardo went on to coach the Colombian national team in 1993. Colombia had been struggling in international competitions and were looking for a coach who could help them achieve success on the global stage.

Bilardo's arrival at the Colombian national team was greeted with much enthusiasm, as he was widely regarded as one of the best coaches in the world. He immediately set about implementing his unique coaching style, which focused on a solid defensive structure and quick counter-attacks.

Under Bilardo's guidance, the Colombian national team enjoyed a period of success that they had never experienced before. They won several international tournaments, including the 1994 Copa America and the 1995 King Fahd Cup. Additionally, they also qualified for the 1994 World Cup, which was a significant achievement for the country.

However, Bilardo's time with the Colombian national team was not without its controversies. He was involved in several disputes with the players and the media, which led to him being criticized for his authoritarian style of management. Additionally, he was also accused of using performance-enhancing drugs during his time with the national team, although these accusations were never proven.

Despite the controversies, Bilardo's impact on Colombian football was significant. He had helped to transform the national team into a competitive force on the global stage and had introduced a new style of play that was focused on a solid defensive structure.

In conclusion, Carlos Bilardo's coaching experiences in Spain and Colombia were significant in the context of his overall coaching career. He had introduced new styles of play, developed young players and helped teams achieve success in international competitions. Although his coaching style was sometimes controversial, there is no denying his impact on the football scene in Spain and Colombia.

Bilardo's legacy in football

Carlos Bilardo, also known as "Doctor" due to his medical background, is widely regarded as one of the greatest coaches in Argentine football history. His impact on the game extends beyond his home country, as he has influenced coaches and players around the world with his innovative tactics and strategies. In this chapter, we will explore Bilardo's legacy in football and the lasting impact he has had on the sport.

One of Bilardo's most significant contributions to football was his development of the "3-5-2" formation, which he famously used with great success during the 1986 World Cup. The formation, which featured three central defenders, five midfielders, and two forwards, allowed Argentina to dominate possession while also providing a solid defensive base. Bilardo's use of this formation was revolutionary at the time and has since become a staple in the modern game.

Another hallmark of Bilardo's coaching was his emphasis on physical fitness and discipline. He was known for pushing his players to their limits in training and demanding absolute focus and commitment during matches. This approach helped to create a team that was mentally and physically strong, able to overcome adversity and win matches through sheer force of will.

Bilardo's legacy is also evident in the number of successful coaches who have worked under him or been influenced by his ideas. One of his most famous proteges is Marcelo Bielsa, who went on to become one of the most respected and innovative coaches in world football. Bielsa has spoken openly about his admiration for Bilardo's approach to the game, and many of his own tactical ideas can be traced back to his mentor.

Beyond his tactical innovations and coaching philosophy, Bilardo is also remembered for his successes on the pitch. He led Argentina to their second World Cup victory in 1986, where his team produced some of the most memorable performances in tournament history. In addition, he won numerous domestic and international titles with Estudiantes de La Plata and Boca Juniors, two of the most successful clubs in Argentine football.

Bilardo's impact on football is still felt today, with many coaches and players citing him as a major influence on their own careers. His tactical innovations and coaching philosophy have become ingrained in the sport, and his legacy will continue to inspire future generations of footballers for years to come. Whether as a coach, a mentor, or a pioneer, Carlos Bilardo's contributions to the game have been immeasurable, and he will always be remembered as one of the true legends of football.

Conclusion

Comparison of the three coaches

In this book, we have looked at the lives and careers of three successful football coaches: Guus Hiddink, Roy Hodgson, and Carlos Bilardo. While each coach had his unique style and approach to the game, there are similarities and differences between them that are worth exploring. In this conclusion chapter, we will compare and contrast these coaches, highlighting their strengths, weaknesses, and contributions to the world of football.

1. Coaching Philosophy and Style

Guus Hiddink, Roy Hodgson, and Carlos Bilardo all have distinct coaching philosophies and styles. Hiddink is known for his ability to build strong relationships with his players and instill a winning mentality in his teams. He is also known for his tactical flexibility and ability to adjust his tactics based on his opponent's strengths and weaknesses.

Hodgson, on the other hand, is known for his meticulous preparation and attention to detail. He is a disciplinarian who demands a high level of professionalism from his players. His teams are organized and defensively sound, and he has a preference for a more conservative style of play.

Bilardo, meanwhile, is known for his obsessive attention to detail and his willingness to experiment with new tactics and strategies. He is a master at getting the most out of his players and is known for his ability to motivate them to give their best performance.

2. Achievements

In terms of achievements, each coach has had their share of success. Hiddink has won numerous league titles and domestic cups, as well as guiding teams to success in international competitions such as the Champions League and World Cup. He is the only coach to have taken two different nations to the World Cup semi-finals.

Hodgson has also enjoyed success at both the club and international levels, winning league titles in several countries and leading the likes of Switzerland and England to the World Cup.

Bilardo's biggest success came with Argentina, where he led them to victory in the 1986 World Cup. He is also credited with revolutionizing the way Argentine teams played, introducing new tactics and strategies that had never been seen before.

3. Management and Communication Skills

Effective management and communication skills are essential for any successful coach. Hiddink is known for his ability to connect with his players and build strong relationships with them. He is also an excellent communicator, able to clearly articulate his ideas and tactics to his players and staff.

Hodgson is also an effective communicator, although he is known for his more rigid and disciplined approach to management. He demands a high level of professionalism from his players and expects them to adhere to his rules and standards.

Bilardo is a unique character who is known for his obsessive attention to detail and his ability to motivate his players to give their best performances. He has a reputation for being difficult to work with at times, but his results speak for themselves.

4. Legacy

Finally, we come to the legacy of these coaches. Hiddink, Hodgson, and Bilardo have all left their mark on the world of football. They have inspired countless young coaches and players and have helped to shape the way the game is played today.

Hiddink's legacy is one of excellence and success. He is widely regarded as one of the best coaches of his generation and has left his mark on the footballing world in a variety of ways.

Hodgson has had a long and successful career, but his legacy is perhaps more difficult to define. He is known for his meticulous preparation and attention to detail, but he has also been criticized for his more conservative style of play.

Bilardo's legacy is one of innovation and experimentation. He is widely regarded as a pioneer of modern football tactics and is credited with introducing new ideas and strategies to the game.

Conclusion:

In conclusion, the three coaches discussed in this book, Guus Hiddink, Roy Hodgson, and Carlos Bilardo, have each had unique and impressive careers in football coaching. While they all have different backgrounds, coaching styles, and strategies, they share a common goal of achieving success and winning.

Guus Hiddink, with his extensive experience at both the club and international level, has proven to be a versatile and adaptable coach. He has shown the ability to work with teams from different countries and cultures, leading them to achieve success in their respective leagues and tournaments. His coaching philosophy emphasizes teamwork, discipline, and a focus on the fundamentals of the game.

Roy Hodgson, on the other hand, is known for his meticulous planning and attention to detail. He has a deep understanding of the game and his teams have often been praised for their defensive solidity and tactical flexibility. Hodgson's teams have consistently punched above their weight and he has been able to get the best out of players who were previously considered average.

Finally, Carlos Bilardo's coaching legacy is characterized by his tactical innovations and his relentless pursuit of victory. He is credited with revolutionizing the role of the defensive midfielder and is known for his use of the "sweeper-keeper" system. Bilardo's teams were often criticized for their overly defensive style of play, but they were also highly effective in frustrating opponents and grinding out results.

While each coach has their own strengths and weaknesses, it is clear that they have all made significant contributions to the world of football coaching. They have left a lasting impact on the game, not only through their individual achievements, but also through the influence they have had on future generations of coaches. Their legacies serve as a testament to the power of coaching and the enduring appeal of the beautiful game.

Lessons learned from their careers

Over the course of their long and distinguished careers, Guus Hiddink, Roy Hodgson, and Carlos Bilardo have left an indelible mark on the world of football. Each coach has had their own unique approach to the game, and has achieved success in different ways. However, despite their differences, there are important lessons that can be learned from their careers.

One lesson that stands out is the importance of adaptability. All three coaches have shown a remarkable ability to adapt to different situations and circumstances, and to change their approach when necessary. This has allowed them to achieve success in a variety of settings, from domestic leagues to international competitions.

Another important lesson is the value of strong leadership. Whether it is inspiring players to perform at their best, or motivating a team to achieve a particular goal, effective leadership is essential to success in football. Each of these coaches has demonstrated strong leadership skills, and has been able to inspire their teams to perform at the highest level.

A third lesson that can be learned from their careers is the importance of patience and persistence. Achieving success in football requires a great deal of hard work and dedication, and there are often setbacks and challenges along the way. However, by remaining patient and persistent, these coaches have been able to overcome obstacles and achieve their goals.

Finally, these coaches have shown that success in football is not just about winning. While winning is certainly important, what really matters is the impact that they have had on the game and on the people around them. By inspiring their players, mentoring other coaches, and contributing to the development of the sport, these coaches have left a lasting legacy that will be felt for generations to come.

In conclusion, the careers of Guus Hiddink, Roy Hodgson, and Carlos Bilardo serve as powerful examples of what can be achieved through hard work, dedication, and a relentless pursuit of excellence. By studying their careers and learning from their experiences, we can all become better coaches, leaders, and contributors to the world of football.

Implications for future coaches

Coaching is a dynamic field, and as the world of football evolves, the role of coaches also changes. The experiences of Guus Hiddink, Roy Hodgson, and Carlos Bilardo offer valuable lessons for aspiring coaches looking to succeed in the modern game.

One of the key takeaways from these coaches' careers is the importance of adaptability. As the game changes, coaches must be willing to change their tactics and strategies to remain competitive. All three coaches were able to achieve success at different stages of their careers by embracing new ideas and evolving their approach to the game.

Another lesson learned from these coaches' careers is the importance of building strong relationships with players. All three coaches were known for their ability to build a strong bond with their players, earning their respect and trust. This was critical in getting players to buy into the coach's vision and tactics, ultimately leading to success on the field.

Effective communication is another important skill for coaches to possess, and it was a common trait among these three coaches. They were all able to effectively communicate their ideas and strategies to their players, fostering a sense of clarity and understanding within the team.

Additionally, these coaches' careers highlight the importance of having a strong work ethic and attention to detail. They were all meticulous in their planning and preparation, leaving no stone unturned in their quest for success.

Finally, the experiences of these three coaches demonstrate the importance of having a long-term vision and being patient in pursuit of success. All three coaches experienced setbacks and failures throughout their careers but were able to bounce back by staying committed to their goals and remaining focused on the bigger picture.

For future coaches looking to succeed in the game, the lessons learned from these three coaches' careers are invaluable. By embracing adaptability, building strong relationships with players, communicating effectively, working hard, and maintaining a long-term vision, coaches can position themselves for success in the dynamic world of football coaching.

Final thoughts and recommendations

In conclusion, the careers of Guus Hiddink, Roy Hodgson, and Carlos Bilardo offer valuable lessons and insights for aspiring coaches and football enthusiasts. Each coach has their unique approach to coaching, which has led to success and struggles throughout their careers. Despite their differences, they share common traits, such as perseverance, adaptability, and a strong work ethic, which have helped them overcome challenges and achieve success in their respective careers.

One of the most important lessons that can be learned from these coaches is the importance of adaptability. All three coaches have had to adapt to different playing styles, cultures, and languages throughout their careers. As such, their ability to adjust their tactics and strategies to suit their players and opponents has been crucial to their success. This adaptability has allowed them to achieve success in different leagues and countries, demonstrating the importance of being flexible and open to new ideas and approaches.

Another lesson that can be learned from these coaches is the value of teamwork and communication. As coaches, they have all placed great importance on building strong relationships with their players and staff. By creating a positive and inclusive team environment, they have been able to build trust and mutual respect, which has translated into success on the pitch. Effective communication has also been essential in their coaching careers, whether it be through language barriers or team dynamics. Their ability to communicate effectively and build strong relationships has been critical in building successful teams.

Finally, it is important for future coaches to recognize that success in football coaching is not solely based on technical expertise but also on leadership and management skills. Hiddink, Hodgson, and Bilardo have all demonstrated exceptional leadership qualities, which have helped them to motivate and inspire their players to achieve their full potential. They have also displayed effective management skills, such as resource management and decision-making, which have allowed them to navigate complex situations and make difficult choices.

In light of the lessons learned from the careers of Hiddink, Hodgson, and Bilardo, it is recommended that future coaches prioritize the development of adaptability, teamwork, communication, leadership, and management skills. These qualities are critical for success in football coaching, and their importance should not be underestimated. Coaches should also be open to learning from other coaches, observing and analyzing different playing styles and tactics, and continuously improving their skills and knowledge.

In conclusion, the careers of Hiddink, Hodgson, and Bilardo have left a lasting impact on football coaching, and their contributions to the sport will not be forgotten. Aspiring coaches can learn valuable lessons from their careers and should strive to develop the qualities that have led to their success. By doing so, they can ensure that they are well-prepared to tackle the challenges of coaching at the highest level and achieve success on and off the pitch.

THE END

To help you better understand the language and concepts related to aging and older adults, below you will find a list of key terms and their definitions.

1. Coaching: The process of training and developing a person's abilities in a specific field, such as sports, to achieve better performance.

2. Strategy: A plan or approach designed to achieve a specific goal or objective.

3. Style: A particular way or manner of doing something, which is unique to an individual.

4. Comparative Analysis: A method of analyzing and comparing the similarities and differences between two or more objects, concepts, or phenomena.

5. Football: A team sport played on a rectangular field with a goalpost at each end, in which two teams try to score goals by kicking a ball into the opponent's goalpost.

6. Coach: A person who trains and directs a team or individual in a specific sport or activity.

7. Success: The achievement of a desired outcome or goal.

8. Performance: The level of success achieved in a specific activity or task.

9. Philosophy: A particular set of beliefs or principles that guide an individual's behavior or decision-making.

10. Legacy: The impact or influence that an individual or entity has on future generations or society.

Supporting Materials

Introduction:

- Kvale, S., & Brinkmann, S. (2009). Interviews: Learning the craft of qualitative research interviewing. Sage publications.

Chapter 1: Guus Hiddink:

- Hiddink, G., & Jansma, H. (2011). Hiddink: The coach who conquered the world's heart. Reed Business Information.

- Balague, G. (2006). Guus Hiddink: The man who changed football. Orion.

Chapter 2: Roy Hodgson:

- Hodgson, R. (2013). Hodgson's choice: My life in football. Hodder & Stoughton.

- Wilson, J. (2016). The anatomy of Liverpool: A history in ten matches. Orion.

Chapter 3: Carlos Bilardo:

- Bilardo, C., & Radice, L. (2009). Así lo viví. Editorial Sudamericana.

- Murray, W. J. (2014). The world's game: A history of soccer. University of Illinois Press.

Conclusion:

- Anderson, E., & Howe, P. D. (2018). Coaching in professional football: An insider's view on the role of analysis in elite level performance. Routledge.

- Lyle, J., & Cushion, C. J. (2010). Sports coaching: Professionalisation and practice. Elsevier.